SPACE

SPACE

ROBERT GARDNER

DRAWINGS BY DORIS ETTLINGER

TWENTY-FIRST CENTURY BOOKS

A DIVISION OF HENRY HOLT AND COMPANY / NEW YORK

Twenty-First Century Books
A Division of Henry Holt and Company, Inc.
115 West 18th Street
New York, NY 10011

Henry Holt® and colophon are trademarks of
Henry Holt and Company, Inc.
Publishers since 1866

Text Copyright © 1994 by Robert Gardner
All rights reserved.
Published in Canada by Fitzhenry & Whiteside Ltd.,
195 Allstate Parkway, Markham, Ontario L3R 2T8

Library of Congress Cataloging-in-Publication Data
Gardner, Robert, 1929–
Space / Robert Gardner.—ed.
p.   cm.—(Yesterday's science, today's technology)
Includes index.
1. Space Sciences—Experiments—Juvenile literature.
2. Astronautics—Experiments—Juvenile literature.
3. Astronomy—Study and teaching.   4. Science—Study and teaching.
[1. Space sciences—Experiments.   2. Experiments.]
1. Title   II. Series: Gardner, Robert, 1929-
Yesterday's science, today's technology.
QB500.22.G37   1994
500.5—dc20   93-38521
                                                            CIP
                                                            AC
ISBN 0-8050-2851-X
First edition—1994

Printed in Mexico
All first editions are printed on acid-free paper ∞.

1   3   5   7   9   10   8   6   4   2

Photo Credits

Cover: © National Aeronautics and Space Administration (NASA); p. 10: © NASA; p. 13:
© George East/Science Photo Library/Photo Researchers Inc.; p. 17: © NASA; p. 30:
© Bob Emmott; p. 50: © NASA; p. 60: © NASA; p. 63: © NASA; p. 69: © NASA

CONTENTS

INTRODUCTION

The second half of the twentieth century marks the beginning of the space age. It was in 1957 that the USSR launched Sputnik, the world's first artificial satellite. Three and a half years later, on April 12, 1961, the same country sent a spaceship (Vostok I) carrying Yuri Gagarin into orbit. Gagarin became the first human to orbit the earth.

Earthbound satellites were followed by rockets to the moon. Some of these spacecraft made soft landings on the lunar surface and sent back pictures of the moon's landscape. Later, lunar satellites orbited the moon and photographed the back side of the moon, which had never been seen before. On July 20, 1969, United States astronaut Neil Armstrong became the first human to set foot on the moon as he uttered his famous words, "That's one small step for man, one giant leap for mankind."

While we have made amazing progress in space science since World War II, it may surprise you to learn that the science underlying these achievements had existed for nearly 300 years. What was lacking was the technology—the means of applying the science in a practical way. Sir Isaac Newton (1642–1727) knew that the moon was an earth satellite. He knew too why the moon stayed in orbit around the earth. He even explained how one might launch an artificial satellite from a very high mountain provided the satellite could be made to move with a speed of 29,000 kilometers per hour (kph), or 18,000 mph. Of course, in the seventeenth century, no one knew how to make anything go that fast. Nor did people know how to survive in the vacuum found in the space above earth's atmosphere. It took 300 years before the technology needed to reach such speeds and endure an airless environment was developed. Only then were humans able to enter the vast space beyond the earth's atmosphere.

Some may question why we should spend money on space programs; others wonder why we don't spend more. The basic reason for space exploration is curiosity. Humans have always wondered what's out there. Satellites, space probes, and space stations provide vast amounts of information not only about space, the solar system, and the universe beyond, but about the earth as well. Space is our new frontier. Having conquered most of earth's frontiers, we now reach out into space, to a frontier that extends for distances yet unknown.

In addition, there have been major so-called spin-offs as a result of space exploration—useful and practical technologies developed for space that have found other uses in our daily lives. For example, the microelectronic devices found in computers, cars, and various appliances were first developed for use in space, as were a variety of miniature gadgets now used in medicine and elsewhere. The anticorrosion, nonflammable, nontoxic, water-based paints that were developed to protect space vehicles and launchers are now used on bridges, pipelines, ships, and oil rigs. Even Teflon-coated pans and Velcro, so common on clothing and footwear today, were first developed for use in space.

Some anthropologists and sociologists believe that stagnant cultures—ancient Rome, for example—dissolve from within. They tend to feed on the past and ignore the future. Space offers a challenge for the future and a way to continue to develop our culture. It may also serve as a means of bringing countries together, breaking national barriers, and uniting all humans in a common quest. In fact, NASA's plans for a space station already include the participation of other countries. Together, Russian and American space scientists are beginning to formulate plans for a manned landing on Mars early in the twenty-first century.

Those who have made the journey into space recognize the fragility of earth and its inhabitants. Perhaps the greatest accomplishment of space exploration will be to make us more aware of how small earth really is, how limited are its resources, and how casual has been our treatment of its land, water, and atmosphere.

In this book, you will investigate some of the scientific principles and technology involved in space science. Each chapter contains a number of activities designed to enhance your understanding of the subject. You will find a ✖ beside a few of the activities. The ✖ indicates that you should ask an adult to help you because the activity may involve an action or the use of something that might be dangerous. Be sure to find adult help before attempting activities marked in this way.

Some of the activities, which are preceded by a ★, might be appropriate starting points for a science fair project. Bear in mind, however, that judges at such contests are looking for original ideas and creative thinking. Projects copied from a book are not likely to impress anyone. However, you may find that one or more of the activities in this book will stimulate a project or experiment of your own design that will lead you to the winner's circle at your school's next science or invention fair.

1

OBSERVING THE SPACE AROUND US

If we watch the sky, which is our window into space, we see that the sun, moon, planets, and stars appear to move around us. Every day these space-bound bodies rise in the east, move across the sky, and set in the west. Their rising and setting times change from day to day to be sure, and their paths shift from season to season. But it appears to us, as it did to the first humans, that these brightly shining bodies move around the earth. In fact, if you were to call someone on the opposite side of the earth at midnight, they would tell you that the sun was at its highest point in the sky and was still moving from east to west.

Of course, in saying that the sun, moon, and stars move around the earth, you probably assumed that the earth is a sphere. Photographs taken from spacecraft leave little doubt about the earth's shape. Before these photographs, however, people had to rely on more subtle evidence about the earth's shape.

A view of the earth taken from the Apollo 12 spacecraft on its second lunar landing mission

EARTH'S SHADOW

MATERIALS
- *light bulb*
- *dark room with light-colored wall*
- *ball*
- *disk*
- *cylinder*
- *cone*
- *objects with various shapes*

One piece of evidence related to the earth's shape has to do with the shadow it casts. Turn on a single light bulb at one end of a dark room. Hold a ball near a wall at the other end of the room. What is the shape of the ball's shadow?

The earth casts a shadow because the sun shines on it. Normally, we can't see the earth's shadow, but sometimes it's visible on the surface of the moon, which is only about 380,000 kilometers (240,000 miles) away. When this happens, sunlight that normally reaches the moon is blocked by the earth. We call it a lunar eclipse. The photograph shows the moon moving into earth's shadow. What evidence do you see from the photograph to suggest that the earth is a sphere?

Does the photograph prove that the earth is a sphere? Before you answer this question, return to the darkened room with its light bulb. Can you cast a round shadow on the wall using a disk? Using a cylinder, such as a tin can? Using a cone? Can you cast round shadows using any other object?

Does the shape of the earth's shadow alone prove that the earth is a sphere? What other evidence suggests that the earth is a sphere? Is there any evidence to suggest that it has some other shape?

The moon is shadowed by the earth during a partial lunar eclipse.

Copernicus and Another Point of View

For thousands of years, people thought the earth was at rest. They believed the sun, moon, planets, and stars went around the earth every day. The idea that the earth is the center or point about which the rest of the universe moves is called the *geocentric*, or earth-centered, universe.

15

In 1543, Nicolaus Copernicus (1473–1543) published a book suggesting that the motion of the sun, moon, planets, and stars could be explained from a *heliocentric*, or sun-centered, point of view. He pointed out that the movement of the sun, moon, planets, and stars across the sky would appear to be the same if the earth rotated once each day.

ACTIVITY 2

THE EARTH AND
THE SUN—TWO POINTS OF VIEW

MATERIALS
- *dark room*
- *flashlight*
- *person to help you*

Stand in place in a dark room, and look straight ahead. Let your head represent the earth. Now have someone hold a flashlight and point it at you. The flashlight represents the sun. Have that person walk around you in a clockwise (from your left to your right) circular motion keeping the "sun" pointed at you as he or she moves. You will see the "sun" rise on your left and set on your right.

Next, ask the person to stand still so that the "sun" will be at rest and pointed toward the back of your head (the earth). Now turn slowly in place in a counterclockwise manner; that is, turn slowly to your left. On which side of your body do you see the sun rise? On which side does the sun set?

Which of the two motions you have tried represents the geocentric point of view? The heliocentric point of view? In both cases, which way does the sun appear to move?

From either point of view, if the top of your head represents the North Pole, which side of your head represents East? West?

Using a globe, or a large ball, and a flashlight, design a model of your own to show others how either of these two points of view can explain the sun's motion across the sky.

Does the Earth Revolve Around the Sun?

Copernicus suggested, too, that a rotating earth might also be moving in a path (an orbit) about the sun (see Figure 1a). Indeed, he

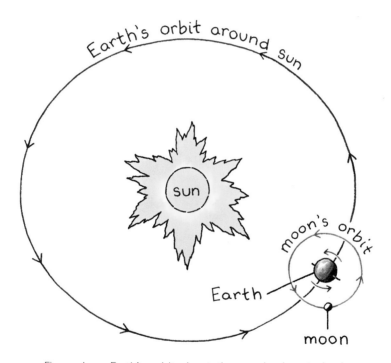

Figure 1: a. Earth's orbit about the sun is almost circular. Notice that the moon orbits the earth as the earth orbits the sun. The drawing is not to scale. The sun is actually about 150,000,000 km (94,000,000 mi) from earth, while the moon is only 386,000 km (240,000 mi) from earth.

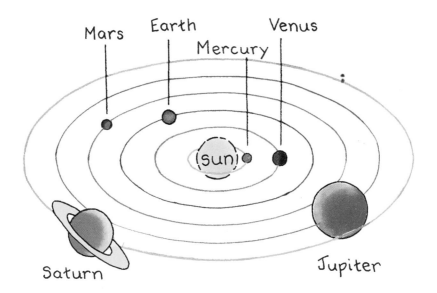

Figure 1: b. The planets of the solar system are shown (not to scale) in orbit about the sun (S). The planets, in order of their distances from the sun, are Mercury, (Me), Venus (V), Earth (E), Mars (Ma), Jupiter (J), and Saturn (Sat). The more distant planets, Uranus, Neptune, and Pluto, are not shown. The table gives the actual distances of the planets from the sun in millions of miles.

suggested that all the planets of our solar system orbited the sun (see Figure 1b). (At that time only Mercury, Venus, Earth, Mars, Jupiter, and Saturn had been discovered. Uranus, Neptune, and Pluto were discovered later). The planets emit no light of their own. They are visible because they reflect sunlight. The sun, which is a star, produces most of the light in the solar system.

The distances shown in Figure 1b may seem huge, but they are very small compared to the distance to the nearest star outside the solar system. That star, Alpha Centauri, is about 4.3 light-years away. A light-year is the distance light travels in one year, which is equal to nearly six trillion (6,000,000,000,000) miles—nearly 1,600 times the distance from the sun to Pluto. The rest of the stars are farther away; some are more than a billion light-years

The constellation Orion includes two nebulae, which are clouds of gas and dust.

The constellation Sagittarius is visible in the Northern Hemisphere on summer nights.

away, so you can see that the solar system occupies but a tiny fraction of all of space. According to the information given here, what is the distance to the nearest star? What is the approximate speed at which light travels in miles per hour (mi/h)? In miles per second (mi/s)? How long does it take light to reach us from the sun?

The earth's motion about the sun explains why we see different constellations (groups of stars) in the winter sky than we do on summer evenings. The first photograph shows the constellation Orion, which shines brightly in the sky on the long nights of winter. The second picture is of the constellation Sagittarius, which is visible on summer nights.

ACTIVITY 3

THE NIGHT SKY ABOVE
AN ORBITING EARTH

MATERIALS
- *shadeless lamp and bulb*
- *sheets of paper*
- *colored pens or crayons*
- *pins or tape*

As the seasons of the year pass, observe the night sky at about the same time in the evening at least several times a month. You will see that the polar constellations (the ones around the North Star), such as the Big Dipper, Cassiopeia, and Cephus, appear to move slowly counterclockwise about the North Star. Other constellations farther from the North Star, such as Orion, Sagittarius, Cygnus, Gemini, and others move slowly westward (counterclockwise) with time (see Figure 2, which also shows you how to locate the North Star).

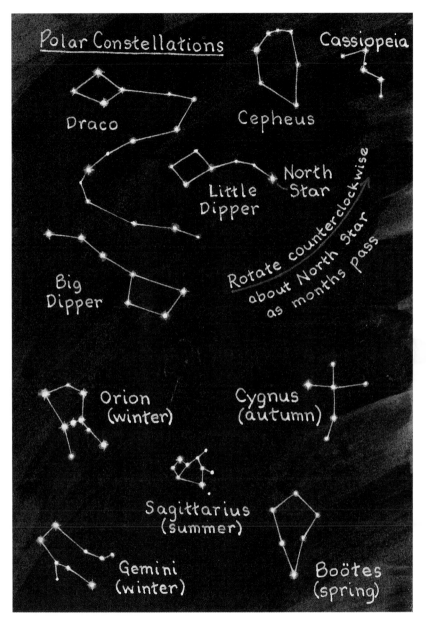

Figure 2. Some prominent constellations visible in the night sky. The polar constellations are visible throughout the year. The others can be seen for only part of the year. Notice how you can use the pointer stars of the Big Dipper to locate the North Star.

You can make a model of the earth in an orbit about the sun and see why the constellations we see change from season to season. A light bulb at the center of an otherwise dark room can represent the sun. Your head can again represent the earth. Draw large diagrams on big sheets of paper to represent different constellations. Tape or pin these drawings of various constellations to different walls in the room. The drawings represent the very distant stars; the ones that are so far away they seem not to move relative to one another.

Walk slowly around the light bulb in the center of the room. Your moving head represents the earth's path around the sun. Stop at one position in your orbit around the "sun." Turn your head away from the "sun." By doing so, you represent the earth's rotation as it orbits the sun. When the "sun" is at your back, your face is turned toward the night "sky." What "constellation" do you see in this "midnight sky?"

Face the "sun" once more and move about one-quarter of the way around the "orbit" (a three-month-long path for the sun). Again, face away from the "sun." What "constellation" is in the "midnight sky" now? Repeat this after moving halfway and three-quarters of the way around the orbit. What "constellations" are visible in each of these "midnight skies"?

How does your model explain why we see a different pattern of stars in the sky as we move from one season to the next?

Using a globe, a shadeless lamp, and objects or drawings to represent distant constellations, design a model of your own to show others how the changing pattern of stars in the earth's night sky can be explained.

What is meant when someone says, "The sun is in Sagittarius," or "The sun is in Aquarius"?

MOTION AND DISTANCE

MATERIALS
- *large field*

If you've ever watched an airplane or a satellite move across the sky, you know that it appears to move much more slowly than nearby objects, such as a car or a pedestrian. The plane or satellite actually moves much faster than an auto or a person, but because it is so far away, it appears to move slowly. It "sweeps out" fewer of a circle's 360 degrees per minute than does a nearer, more slowly moving object.

To examine this effect more closely, stand in the middle of a large field such as a soccer or baseball field. Have one person who is about 10 feet away walk around you in a circle. Have a second person, near the edge of the field several hundred feet away, run around you at this much greater distance. Which person goes around you more times in a minute? Which person sweeps out more degrees of a circle per minute?

Both stars and planets appear to move 360° each day because the earth turns once every 24 hours. Planets were originally thought to be stars, but they "wandered"—their positions in the sky changed relative to the constellations. (In fact, the word *planet* comes from a Greek word meaning "wanderer.") As you know, the stars that make up the constellations are very far away.

Why, even after hundreds of years, do constellations appear not to move relative to one another?

Why do the planets change position relative to these constellations?

Does the Earth Turn?

People resisted Copernicus's heliocentric idea because for centuries everyone had assumed that the earth was the center of the universe. As you have seen, the motion of the sun, moon, and stars can be explained using either a geocentric or a heliocentric point of view. Gradually, evidence suggested that the heliocentric model was the better of the two, but no one could prove that the earth rotates. It was not until after Sir Isaac Newton had developed his laws of motion and the idea of gravity that anyone could show that the earth really does rotate. You'll learn about Newton's laws and gravity in the next chapter. Then we'll return to the question: Does the earth turn?

2

NEWTON, MOTION, AND GRAVITY

Like all good scientists, Newton built his ideas on foundations established by others. He was well aware of this fact when he wrote: "If I have seen further than other men, it is because I stood on the shoulders of giants."

One of these giants was Galileo Galilei (1564–1642). In fact, the basis for Newton's first law of motion came from Galileo. It was he who first realized that an object in motion will continue moving in the same direction and at the same speed unless a force (a push or a pull) is applied to it. Before Galileo, people assumed that a force was needed to keep an object moving. But Galileo realized that it was friction—the force between two surfaces rubbing together—that opposed motion and caused most moving objects to come to rest. The force needed to keep ordinary objects in motion is simply the force needed to overcome friction.

Galileo realized that without friction a moving object would continue to move forever. He described ramps like the ones in Figure 3 to illustrate his point. He reasoned that without friction, a ball sliding down the left-hand ramp will rise to the same height on the right-hand ramp and back up the left-hand ramp. If you gradually lengthen the right-hand ramp, the ball will move farther and farther. If the right-hand ramp were eliminated and the ball allowed to slide on an infinitely long plane, it would move at a steady speed forever.

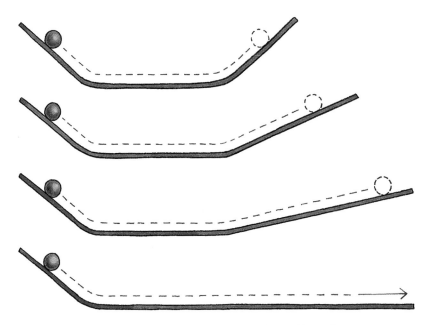

Figure 3. Galileo's way of illustrating motion without force

GALILEO AND THE FIRST LAW
OF MOTION—PART I

MATERIALS
- *long string or thread*
- *large metal washers*
- *tape*
- *yardstick, meter stick, or ruler*

By making a pendulum, you can see why Galileo believed that a moving object will continue to move forever unless a force changes its motion. Build a pendulum using the drawing in Figure 4 to guide you. Make your first pendulum about 25 cm (10 in.) long. Pull the pendulum bob (washers) to one side until it is about 1 cm (1/2 in.) higher than it was when at rest. Then release it. How far horizontally does the pendulum move with each swing?

Now make the pendulum 100 cm or 1 m (40 in.) long. Again, move the bob to the side until it is about 1 cm (1/2 in.) higher than it was when at rest and release it. How far horizontally does this pendulum move with each swing? If possible, make the pendulum 2 m (80 in.) long. How far horizontally does this pendulum move with each swing?

What happens to the distance the pendulum bob moves horizontally as you make the pendulum longer and longer? Does the pendulum return to the same height from which you released it? To find out, pull the pendulum bob to one

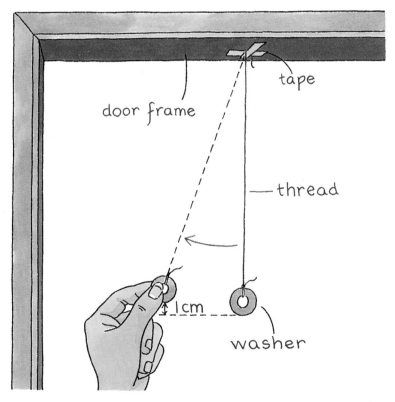

Figure 4. A simple pendulum moves with very little friction.

side. Put your nose on the bob before you release it. (Caution: Be sure you release it; don't push it.) Keep your nose in that same place until the pendulum bob returns. Does it come back to very nearly the same point from which you released it? Why will the pendulum eventually come to rest? If there were no friction in the pendulum, how long do you think it would swing? How long did Galileo think it would swing?

GALILEO AND THE FIRST LAW
OF MOTION—ANOTHER LOOK

MATERIALS
- *long string or thread*
- *metal washers*
- *tape*
- *yardstick, meter stick, or ruler*
- *air hockey game (optional)*
- *square piece of 6-mm (1/4-in.) plywood 7.5 cm (3 in.) on a side*
- *drill*
- *1.5-mm (1/16-in.) bit*
- *empty thread spool*
- *wood glue*
- *large balloon*

There are other ways to see why Galileo believed that bodies would continue to move forever in the absence of force. One way is to play with the puck on an air hockey game. What happens to the puck when you give it a small push? Does it stop, or does it continue to move with no significant loss of speed?

If you don't have an air hockey game, you can build a nearly frictionless air car like the one shown in Figure 5. Ask an adult to help you cut a 7.5-cm (3-in.) square from a piece of 6-mm (1/4 in.) thick plywood. Also ask the adult to help you drill a 1.5-mm (1/16-inch) hole in the center of the square. Use sandpaper to smooth the wood and round the edges. Then glue an empty thread spool over the hole. Be sure the hole in the spool is in line with the hole in the square.

When the glue has dried, blow up a large balloon, twist its neck, and attach it to the spool as shown. Place your air car on a smooth level surface such as a Formica counter and give it a push. What do you have to do to change the motion of the air car? How does the air car illustrate the first law of motion? How can you use your air car to determine whether a surface is level or slightly tilted?

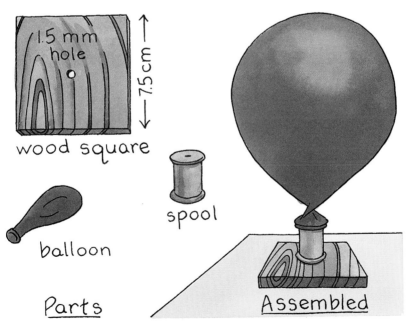

Figure 5. An air car moves with very little friction.

THE FIRST LAW
OF MOTION—PART 2

MATERIALS
- *plastic cup*
- *water*
- *sheet of smooth paper*
- *smooth counter or table*
- *ball*
- *wagon, large enough to sit in*
- *playing card*
- *marble*
- *narrow-mouth jar*

As you have seen, a body in motion will maintain its speed and direction of motion unless a force acts on it. The second part of the first law of motion applies when an object's speed is zero. It states that if a body is at rest (not moving), then it will remain at rest unless a force is applied to it. You can illustrate this idea with a magician's trick. Half fill a plastic cup with water. Place the cup on a sheet of very smooth paper near the edge of a smooth, clean counter or table (see Figure 6). Because the surfaces are very smooth, the frictional forces between cup and paper should be quite small. Grasp the edge of the paper and pull it forward and downward with a quick snap. If you pull sharply, the small frictional force cannot act on the cup for very long. Where is the cup after the paper has been pulled?

Another approach is to put a playing card on top of a narrow-mouth jar. Then put a marble on the card over the center of the jar's mouth. Use your fingers to quickly pull the card off the jar. What happens to the marble?

Or you can place a ball in the center of a wagon. If you

Figure 6. A body at rest remains at rest unless acted on by a force.

suddenly give the wagon a strong pull forward, what happens to the ball? How do these activities illustrate the second part of the first law of motion?

You can use the same ball and wagon to show that a body in motion maintains its motion. This time start the wagon very slowly so the ball stays in the center of the wagon. Slowly accelerate the wagon until the wagon and the ball in its center are moving fairly fast. Then suddenly stop the wagon. What happens to the ball? How does this last experiment help you to understand why you should wear seat belts when riding in a car?

Suppose you were in a spaceship far from any planets or stars. If the ship had all its motors off and was headed toward a small, distant star trillions of kilometers away at a speed of 20,000 km/s (12,420 mi/s), what would be its speed and direction an hour later?

Aerial view of the Foucault pendulum at the Franklin Institute
Science Museum in Philadelphia

Now that you know about the first law of motion, we can return to the question: Does the earth turn? This question was answered in the nineteenth century by a French scientist, Jean Foucault (1819–1868).

Foucault reasoned that a swinging pendulum should maintain its plane of swing. The pendulum moves because gravity pulls the bob downward. But there is no force pushing the bob sideways; therefore, the direction of the bob's motion should not change. He realized that if the earth were rotating, the plane of a pendulum's swing should *appear* to change. At the North Pole, this rotation would be a full circle, 360°, in 24 hours; the earth would be turning under the pendulum whose direction of motion would not change. Farther south, the rotation would be less; at the equator, there would appear to be no rotation. When Foucault performed the experiment, using a long pendulum with a very heavy bob and minimal friction, he found that the plane of swing did indeed appear to rotate.

You may have seen this experiment at a science museum. If not, the next activity is a model of such a pendulum.

ACTIVITY 8

A MODEL OF
A FOUCAULT PENDULUM

MATERIALS
- *long string or thread*
- *metal washers*
- *tape*
- *large lazy Susan*

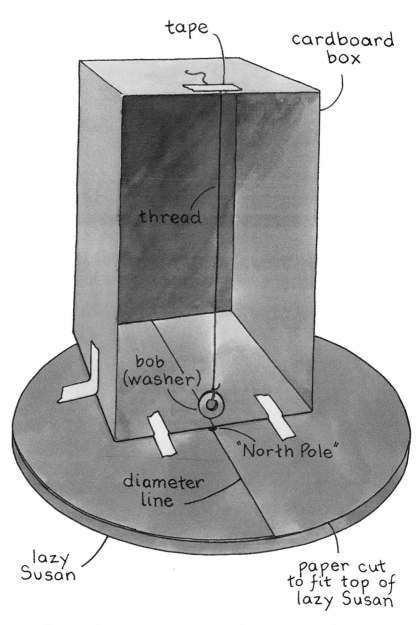

Figure 7. A model of a Foucault pendulum at the North Pole

Cut a piece of paper to fit the top of the lazy Susan. Draw a straight line along a diameter of the paper. Hang a pendulum from a small box (see Figure 7). Tape the box to the lazy Susan so that the motionless pendulum hangs over the center of the lazy Susan. Draw a line along the diameter of the paper and extend it into the box as shown. The center of the diameter line under the motionless bob represents the earth's North Pole. Set the pendulum in motion back and forth just above the diameter line. Now turn the lazy Susan very slowly and gently to represent a slowly turning earth at the North Pole. If you were at the North Pole, would the plane of swing of a moving pendulum appear to rotate? What would this answer tell you?

The Second Law of Motion

Once Newton accepted Galileo's idea of inertia (the first law of motion), he turned to the question of what happens when a force *is* applied to an object. You can gain some understanding of the second law by carrying out the next activity.

 ACTIVITY 9

THE EFFECT OF
FORCE ON MOTION

MATERIALS
- *thread*
- *block of wood*
- *small metal washers*
- *2 thumbtacks*

■ *paper clip or pulley*
■ *smooth board about 20-30 cm (8-12 in.) wide and .6-.9 m (2-3 ft.) long*
■ *sandpaper*

To see what effect a force has on an object, you can attach a long thread to a block and use washers hung from the other end of the thread to pull on the block as shown in Figure 8. The block should be smooth so that it will slide easily along the smooth board. If you don't have such a block, ask an adult to help you make some by cutting a 5-cm by 10-cm (2-in. x 4-in.)

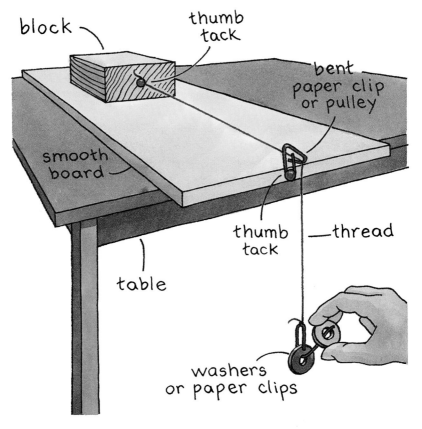

Figure 8. When a force greater than the force needed to overcome friction acts on a block, how does it move?

board into 10-cm (4-in.) lengths. Then you can use sandpaper to make them smooth. The blocks will be useful for other activities as well.

Begin by hanging just enough small washers on the string so that when you tap the end of the board, the block moves at a steady speed. If the block moves at a constant speed in a fixed direction, the total force on the block must be zero because its motion is not changing. The force applied to the block is just enough to balance the frictional force that opposes its motion. The net force on the block is zero because the force pulling the block forward is just equal to the frictional force opposing the motion. If you wanted to measure these forces, you could use a spring balance. You would find that forces are measured in units called newtons (N) in the metric system, or in units called pounds (lb) or ounces (oz) in the English system.

Now use twice as many washers to pull the block as you used to overcome friction. In this way, you can be sure that there will be a net force on the block—a force greater than that needed to overcome friction. What happens to the block's speed as it is pulled by the net force?

ACTIVITY 10

ACCELERATION,
AN ACCELEROMETER, AND FORCES

MATERIALS
- *accelerometer—small carpenter's level or clear, tall 5-7.5 cm (2-3 in.) watertight vial*
- *water*
- *small piece of soap*
- *materials used in Activity 9, plus a second block of wood*
- *clear tape*

In the previous experiment, you saw a block's speed increase as it was pulled by a force. When an object's speed increases, we say that it accelerates. If its speed decreases, we say it decelerates. Pushing on a car's accelerator causes the car to accelerate. Pushing on a car's brake pedal causes it to decelerate.

An accelerometer is a device that indicates acceleration and the direction of the acceleration. Because an acceleration is always in the direction of the force causing the acceleration, an accelerometer also indicates the direction of a force. You can use a small carpenter's level as an accelerometer, or you can build one by filling a tall, clear vial with water (see Figure 9a). Add a tiny piece of soap to the vial to reduce the water's surface tension, and leave a small space at the top so that an

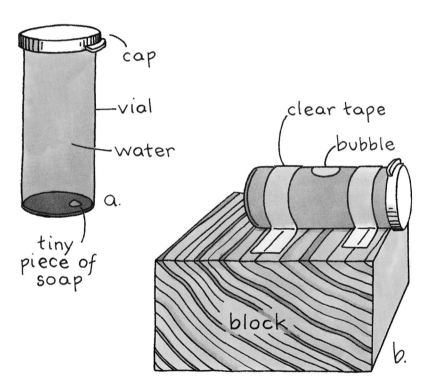

Figure 9: a. An accelerometer can be made from a pill vial. b. An accelerometer attached to a block

38

air bubble will be visible when you cap the vial and turn it on its side.

Place the accelerometer on a smooth table or counter. Watch the accelerometer's air bubble as you accelerate the vial first to the right, then to the left. Notice that the bubble always moves in the direction of the acceleration or deceleration—the direction of the force causing the change in speed.

Tape the accelerometer to the block you used in Activity 9. Be sure it is level so the bubble is at the center of the upper side of the vial (see Figure 9b). Now use enough washers to make the block accelerate. Does the bubble move as you would expect?

Increase the force pulling the block by at least doubling the number of washers. Is the acceleration of the block greater or less than it was before? How can you tell? How does the accelerometer indicate whether the acceleration is large or small?

Place a second block (identical to the first one) under the first block and attach the thread to it. The mass (the amount of matter) being pulled will then be increased. Keep the force the same as in the last trial you ran. How does the additional mass affect the acceleration?

Newton and the Second Law of Motion

From your own experiments, which were similar but less accurate than Newton's, you may already have guessed the second law of motion. When a force acts on an object, its speed changes. If the force is in the direction of the object's motion, the object accelerates. If a force acts against the object's motion, the object's speed decreases and the object decelerates. If the force is doubled, the acceleration (or deceleration) is doubled. If the force is tripled, the acceleration (or deceleration) is tripled, and so on. Furthermore, if the mass (the amount of matter) of the object, which can be measured in units called kilograms (kg) or grams (g), doubles and the force remains the same, the acceleration becomes half as great. If the mass triples, the acceleration becomes one-third as great, and so on.

Forces, Gravity, and Newton

You may have heard the story about Newton discovering gravity when an apple fell on his head. That's not really what happened, but a falling apple did lead him to realize that a force causing motion here on earth could also cause planets and moons to move. The force Newton recognized—the force that holds us all to the earth and keeps the planets in their orbits—is the force of gravity.

If you drop a ball, it falls toward the earth. As you will see, the ball accelerates as it falls, so there must be a force on it. We call that force gravity. It's the force that attracts everything toward the earth, be it leaves, people, cars, or the moon. The few people who have walked on the moon know that the moon exerts a gravitational force, too, one that is about one-sixth as strong as earth's. Gravitational forces exist near all planets, stars, and moons; in fact, everything that has mass exerts a pull on every other mass.

★ **ACTIVITY II**

THE FORCE OF GRAVITY
AND ACCELERATION

MATERIALS
- *ball*
- *tape*
- *grooved ruler*
- *board or book*
- *object about 2 cm (3/4 in.) thick (such as several washers stacked together)*
- *block to put at end of ruler*

You can prove to yourself that a falling object accelerates. First, measure the time it takes a ball to fall 1 m (1 yd). A simple way of timing is to count to five as fast as possible. You'll find it takes just about one second. To check this measurement, count to five as fast as you can ten times in a row. You'll find that it takes about ten seconds. You can even use this method to estimate fractions of a second—each count corresponds to one-fifth of a second.

Hold the ball 1 m (1 yd) above the floor. Begin counting the instant you release the ball. Repeat this process a number of times. You should find that you count only to "two" and are about ready to say "three" when the ball hits the floor. This means it takes between 0.4 and 0.5 second for the ball to reach the floor. Now drop the ball from a height of 2 m (2 yds). If the ball falls at a steady speed, it should take twice as long as it did to fall 1 m, or about 0.9 s. How long does it take for the ball to fall 2 m? Does it take twice as long or less than twice as long? Does the ball accelerate?

If you find these time intervals are too small for you to measure accurately, you can resort to a trick used by Galileo to dilute the effects of gravity. Tape a 30-cm (12-in.) grooved ruler to a flat board or book (see Figure 10). Raise one end of the ruler by putting an object about 2 cm (3/4 in.) thick under the board about 30 cm (12 in.) from the other end. Place a marble in the groove about 13 cm (5 in.) from its lower end. Put an index finger in front of the marble. To release the marble, simply move your finger forward in the direction the ball will roll. Begin counting the instant you release the marble. How many counts does it take the marble to roll to an object, such as a block, at the end of the ruler?

Next, release the marble from a point 26 cm (10 in.) from the end of the ruler. Now how many counts does it take the marble to reach the end of the ruler? How does this experiment show that the marble accelerates as it rolls down the incline?

Figure 10. Diluting gravity in order to reduce the acceleration of a falling object

Would a heavy ball fall with a different acceleration than a lighter ball? You can find out by dropping a tennis ball and a baseball at the same time. Do the balls fall side by side or does the baseball have a greater acceleration than the tennis ball?

If you drop a book and a piece of paper, they do not fall side by side. The paper is so light that friction between the air and the paper is enough to slow the paper's fall. But what happens if you put the paper on the book and drop them as shown in Figure 11? Do they fall with the same acceleration now? How can you explain what you observe?

Figure 11. Will the book and the paper fall with the same acceleration when arranged this way?

Gravity, Acceleration, Mass, and Weight

You have seen that all objects fall with the same acceleration as long as friction with the air is minimal. From the second law of motion, Newton knew that if a force of 10 N is needed to give an object with a mass of 1 kg (1,000 g or 2.2 lbs) a certain acceleration, a force of 20 N would be needed to give a 2-kg (4.4lb) mass the same acceleration. Since all falling bodies accelerate at the same rate, he reasoned that the force of gravity—the force the earth exerts on objects—pulls twice as hard on a 2-kg object as it does on a 1-kg object and ten times as hard on a 10-kg object. In other words, the force of gravity is proportional to the mass. This pull, which is measured in newtons, kilograms-weight, or pounds, is what we mean by weight.

MASS AND WEIGHT

MATERIALS
- *standard masses (100 g, 200 g, 500 g, 1,000 g or 1 kg)*
- *spring balance calibrated in newtons (0 to 20 N)*
- *shoes, books, paperweights, etc.*

Your school probably has a set of standard masses. They can be used with a balance to determine the mass of various objects. Hang a mass of 100 g on the spring balance. What is its weight in newtons? Repeat this procedure for masses ranging from 100 g to 2 kg. What happens to the weight of an object when its mass doubles? When it triples? How does an object's weight in newtons compare with its mass in kilograms? With its mass in grams?

Now weigh various objects such as shoes, books, paperweights, etc., using your spring balance. What is the mass, in kilograms and grams, of each of the objects you weigh?

If you did this same experiment on the moon, the data you collected would look like that in the table below.

THE WEIGHT OF VARIOUS MASSES WHEN WEIGHED ON THE MOON'S SURFACE

Mass (kg)	Weight (N)
0.10	0.16
0.20	0.32
0.50	0.80
0.70	1.12
1.00	1.60
2.00	3.20

On the moon an object's mass is the same as it is on the earth. After all, it has the same amount of matter wherever it is. Is an object's weight on the moon proportional to its mass? How does the weight of an object on the moon compare to the weight of the same object on the earth?

Newton argued that *any* two masses attract each other with a force that is proportional to their masses. He also showed that as the distance between two objects increases, the force of attraction (gravity) decreases. In fact, if the distance doubles, the force becomes only one-fourth as great. About a century after Newton, Henry Cavendish (1731–1810) was able to measure the tiny force between two ordinary masses at different separations. He not only confirmed Newton's ideas about gravity, but he also gave us a way to find the mass of the earth. It turns out to be about six trillion, trillion kilograms.

Normally, we don't notice the force of attraction between two small masses because it is very small compared with the force that the earth exerts on both masses. The force between two 50-kg (110-lb) people 1 m (1 yd) apart is only about 0.00000017 N, whereas each of them is attracted by the earth with a force of almost 500 N.

The Third Law of Motion

Newton realized that if I push you, you automatically push back on me. Our pushes are equal, but in opposite directions. You can see that this is true in several different ways.

PUSH—PUSH BACK:
THE THIRD LAW OF MOTION

MATERIALS
- *ice skates, roller skates, or skateboards*
- *two large, identical toy trucks*
- *pencil*
- *long, thin rubber band*
- *spring-type clothespins*
- *book*
- *tape*
- *toothpick*

When you are on ice or roller skates, ask a friend who is about your size and also on skates to stand facing away from you. While you are both at rest and standing close to each other, tell your friend that you are going to give him or her a push. Then give your friend a push (see Figure 12). What happens? Which way does your friend move? Which way do you move? Did your friend automatically push back on you?

Repeat the experiment, but this time have your friend push on you. What happens? What happens if your friend pushes harder? What happens if you repeat the experiment with an adult who is much heavier than you?

If you don't have skates, you can do a similar experiment while seated on skateboards. What do you find?

Another way to do this experiment is to connect two large, identical toy trucks with a long thin rubber band as shown in Figure 13. Pull the trucks a short distance apart and have a friend place a pencil at a point midway between them. Release both trucks at the same time. Where do they meet?

Repeat the experiment, but tape a book or some other

Figure 12. If I push you, do you automatically push me?

weight to one of the trucks. Where do they meet now when you release them? Which truck moved faster? Which moved slower?

To see what happens when one truck pushes on the other, tape a spring-type clothespin to one of the trucks as shown in Figure 14. Break a toothpick and place it between the jaws of the clothespin so that it holds them open. Place the second truck close to the first one so that it touches the other side of the clothespin. Then ask an adult to burn the short lengths of toothpick so that the clothespin will "explode," pushing the trucks apart. Do the trucks move apart with about the same speed? Did both trucks push on each other but in opposite directions? How do the results differ if you repeat the experiment with a book or some other weight taped to one of the trucks?

More carefully performed experiments show that when one object pushes or pulls on another, the second object pushes or pulls back with a force that is equal but in the opposite direction. Furthermore, the momentum (the mass times the velocity) of the two bodies is equal but opposite in direction. If a large mass pushes on a small mass, the small mass will move in one direction with a large velocity, and the large mass will move in the opposite direction with a small velocity.

rubber
band

Figure 13. A rubber band allows these two trucks to pull on each other. What happens when you release them?

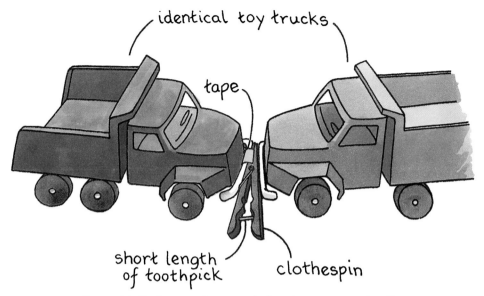

identical toy trucks

tape

short length
of toothpick

clothespin

Figure 14. Taping a spring-type clothespin to one truck will allow the trucks to push on each other.

The third law of motion explains how rocket-powered spacecraft work. Hot gases are forced out of the rocket's exhaust as fuel is burned in its combustion chamber. The rocket, in turn, is pushed in the opposite direction. As the rocket's fuel is burned, its mass decreases. As its mass decreases, each bit of fuel burned gives the rocket a greater acceleration.

Newton's laws of motion are not limited to the earth. As you will see in the next chapter, they explain motions within our solar system and throughout the universe.

3

MOTION IN SPACE

In the Introduction, you learned that Newton developed the science needed to understand satellites. What he lacked was the technology to build and launch these vehicles. The development of that technology began in 1911 with the rocket experiments of Clark University Professor Robert H. Goddard (1882–1945)—experiments that continued until 1930. Goddard used both solid and liquid fuels to power his rockets as he sought a way to explore the upper atmosphere. He realized that rockets, unlike balloons, are not limited in the height to which they can rise. A balloon must be less dense than the air that buoys it upward. The height to which a rocket can ascend is limited only by the fuel it can carry and its own weight.

During World War II, German scientists developed rockets to carry bombs—bombs that exploded on English cities. After the war, many of these same scientists were employed in the United States by the National Aeronautics and Space Administration (NASA) in designing and building rockets to carry satellites and people into space.

Rockets Into Space

The space shuttle is forced into space by two solid-fuel rocket boosters (SRBs) and the spaceship's three main engines. The liquid fuel (hydrogen and oxygen) for the main engines is stored in a huge

external tank (ET) attached to the orbiter—the vehicle carrying the astronauts into space. After the fuel in the SRBs has burned, the empty tanks separate and fall by parachute into the ocean. Later, when the spaceship is nearly out of the atmosphere and the fuel in the ET is gone, this tank is also jettisoned and burns as it falls through the heavier atmosphere below. Beyond this point, about 260 km (160 mi) above the earth, the spaceship's own inboard fuel carries it to a final orbiting altitude.

The mass of a fully fueled rocket divided by the mass of the rocket alone is called the mass ratio. A mass ratio of 2.73 will provide the empty rocket with a final speed equal to that of the burning gases that emerge from the rocket's exhaust nozzle. A mass ratio of 7.45 results in a velocity twice that of the burning fuel. To obtain a final velocity three times that of the exhaust gases, the ratio must be 20.3. To improve the effective mass ratio, most rockets carrying satellites into orbit use multistaging. For example, a rocket may consist of three stages as shown in Figure 15.

The first stage accelerates the rocket through part of its long path into space. When its fuel is gone, it is jettisoned and falls back to earth. This reduces the mass of the rocket and gives it a higher, more favorable mass ratio. The fuel in the second stage is then ignited, accelerating the ship still closer to its orbiting altitude. Again, the second stage is released when its fuel is exhausted, and the third stage is ignited. This stage carries the shuttle and its payload to orbit, reaching a final speed of about 28,500 km/hr (17,700 mi/hr).

Once in orbit, astronauts on board the space shuttle perform a number of experiments and operations related to their mission. One of the shuttle's most important functions is to carry satellites into orbit. Sometimes these satellites are placed in orbits that nearly match the shuttle's orbit. Other times, the satellites carry their own rockets, which are used to lift them into higher orbits.

The launch of the space shuttle *Atlantis* on July 31, 1992

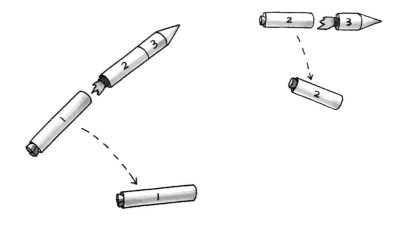

Figure 15. A multistage rocket is an efficient way to send a satellite into orbit. The satellite is carried into orbit by the rocket's final stage. The earlier stages fall back to earth.

A BALLOON ROCKET AND A
MULTISTAGE BALLOON ROCKET

MATERIALS
- *long balloons*
- *twist ties*
- *plastic tape*
- *soda straw*
- *thread*

Blow up a long balloon and seal its mouth with a twist tie. Use plastic tape to attach the balloon to a straw mounted on a long thread (see Figure 16). Move the straw and balloon to the lower end of the long thread. Hold the neck of the balloon as

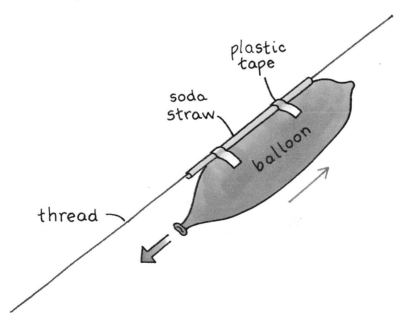

Figure 16. A balloon rocket at "liftoff"

you remove the twist tie. Then release the balloon. What happens? How can you explain what happens?

See if you can use balloons and whatever else you need to build a two-stage or other multistage balloon rocket.

Gravity and Satellites

Once an object has been launched, it is gradually turned so that it moves horizontally as well as vertically. Launches are always from west to east to take advantage of the earth's rotational speed in that direction, which is about 1600 km/hr (1,000 mi/hr) near the equator. When the vehicle reaches the vacuum above our atmosphere and is traveling at nearly 28,500 km/hr (18,000 mi/hr) roughly parallel to the earth's surface, it will be in orbit about the earth. Its orbit may be an ellipse or a circle. But what makes it go around the earth? Why doesn't it continue to move away from the earth?

The answer is that it's not moving fast enough to escape the force of gravity that pulls it toward the earth. If it were moving with a speed of about 40,000 km/hr (25,000 mi/hr), the so-called escape velocity, it could move into deep space and never return to earth. At 28,500 km/hr, it is moving just fast enough so that its speed coupled with its continual fall toward the earth (at an acceleration of nearly 10 m/s every second) just matches the earth's curvature (see Figure 17).

If you partially fill a pail with water and swing it in a circle as you turn in place, you can feel the inward force you have to exert to keep the pail moving in a circle. That inward force that you exert on the pail is called a centripetal force. There must be a centripetal force acting on a satellite, too—a force that keeps it in orbit about the earth. In the case of a satellite, gravity provides the force, and if there's an inward force, there must be an inward acceleration.

In the next activity, you'll see that there really is an inward acceleration when an object moves in a circle. You'll also see what would happen to a satellite if there were no gravity.

Figure 17. A satellite in a circular orbit about the earth has a speed and a rate of fall due to gravity that carries it along a path matching the earth's curvature.

SATELLITE MOTION WITH AND WITHOUT AN INWARD FORCE

MATERIALS
- *accelerometer (see Activity 10)*
- *tape*
- *turntable or lazy Susan*
- *marble*
- *plastic picnic plate or plastic snap-on cover*
- *scissors*

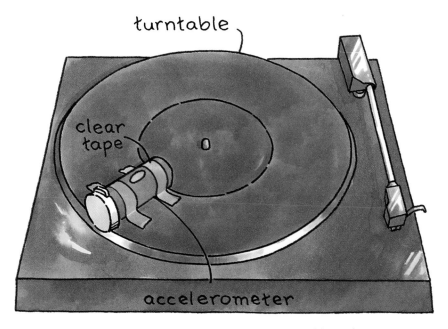

turntable

clear
tape

0

accelerometer

Figure 18. An accelerometer taped to a turntable or lazy
Susan will give you the direction of the acceleration and force
on a body moving in a circle.

Hold the accelerometer you used in Activity 10 in your hand
at arm's length. Be sure the accelerometer is level. Now turn
in a circle. What does the bubble tell you is the direction of
the acceleration? Of the force?

You might also tape your accelerometer to a turntable or a
lazy Susan as shown in Figure 18. When the turntable or lazy
Susan is turning, watch the bubble in the accelerometer. What
is the direction of the acceleration? What is the direction of
the force that keeps the accelerometer moving in a circle?

Suppose you could somehow turn off the force of gravity
that supplies the inward force needed to keep a satellite in
orbit about the earth. Based on your knowledge of the first
law of motion, what would be the satellite's path if the force
of gravity suddenly disappeared?

To check your prediction, roll a marble around the inside

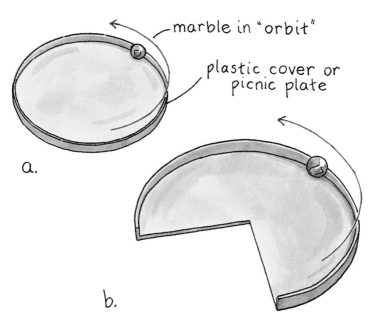

marble in "orbit"

plastic cover or
picnic plate

a.

b.

Figure 19: a. The plate's rim provides the inward (centripetal) force needed to make the marble move in a circle. b. What will happen to the marble when the centripetal force is removed?

of a plastic picnic plate or a plastic snap-on cover as shown in Figure 19a. As you can see, the rim of the plate or cover provides the inward force needed to make the marble move in a circle. Now use scissors to cut away one-quarter of the plate or cover (see Figure 19b). Again, set the marble in motion around the circle's inner circumference. Watch the marble carefully when it reaches the cut-out portion. At this point, the inward force on the marble is missing. Does the marble continue to move in a circle? Does it move outward along a radius of the circle in which it was traveling? Or does it move in a straight line in the direction it was going at the moment the cover's rim stopped pushing on it?

Less than 40 years ago, people marveled at the technology that placed the first satellite in orbit. Today we take satellites for granted, and weather forecasters depend on them. High above the earth's atmosphere, weather satellites constantly relay information and pictures of the earth's clouds and their motion. Satellites monitor thunderstorms, hurricanes, weather fronts, and the jet stream. It is estimated that the improved weather forecasting made possible because of satellites saves farmers at least $2.5 billion each year.

In addition to weather satellites, there are satellites that measure or monitor reflected sunlight, radiation, the earth's magnetic and gravitational fields, ocean currents, ice cover, vegetation, soils, marine life, and land formations. This information enables geographers to develop more accurate and complete maps of the earth's surface.

Early in 1993, a thin umbrella-like plastic mirror on board the Russian spacecraft *Progress* was opened and turned toward the sun. For a period of six minutes, it reflected a weak 4-kilometer- (2.5-mile-) wide beam of light onto the dark continent of Europe. This Russian experiment could be the first step in providing extra wintertime daylight to nothern cities, adding hours of sunlight to the planting and harvesting seasons in agricultural areas and providing light for nighttime rescue operations.

The period of different satellites—the time it takes a satellite to make one trip around the earth—depends on the satellite's orbit. Artificial satellites in orbits close to the earth, such as the space shuttle, have periods of about 80-90 minutes and velocities close to 29,000 km/hr (18,000 mi/hr). The moon, earth's only natural satellite, which has an orbit approximately 60 times the radius of the earth, or about 380,000 km (240,000 mi), has a period of nearly a month and moves around the earth with a velocity of about 3,600 km/hr (2,250 mi/hr).

In between, at a distance of 6.63 earth radii from the earth's center, satellites have a period of 24 hours and speeds of about 11,100 km/hr (6,900 mi/hr). The periods of these satellites match the earth's rotation. Consequently, they will stay in one place above the earth. To us, they appear to be motionless. Syncom (Synchronous Communications) satellites, which have circular orbits above the earth's equator and periods of 24 hours, are used to relay radio, telephone, and television signals around the world.

As a satellite goes into orbit, small rockets are ignited that make it start spinning like a gyroscope or a well-thrown football. If you've ever thrown a football with its wide side leading, you know how unpredictably it moves. By giving it spin, as a good quarterback will do, a football will move along a predictable path. The same is true of Syncom satellites. Furthermore, because there is no air to rub against these satellites, they will continue to spin and maintain their orbits for many years.

★ **ACTIVITY 16**

A MODEL FOR
COMMUNICATION SATELLITES

MATERIALS
- *globe*
- *dark room*
- *penlight*
- *small mirrors*
- *bike*
- *tape*
- *string*

Place a large globe, representing the earth, in a dark room. Turn on a penlight and use it to serve as a beam of radio or television signals sent from some place on the earth. A small mirror held above the globe can be used to represent a

Syncom satellite that reflects the beam back to earth. Signals that would normally escape into space are sent back to earth by the satellite (mirror) (see Figure 20). How many such satellites would be needed to relay signals to almost any place on earth?

To see how a Syncom satellite moves relative to the earth, turn a bicycle on its side or upside down. Mark a point on the hub of the front wheel with a small piece of tape. The hub represents the earth. Run a straight piece of string along a radius from the tape on the hub to a point on the wheel's rim. Put another small piece of tape on the rim at the outer end of the string. This tape represents the position of a Syncom satellite. Now slowly rotate the wheel. Notice how the "earth" and the "satellite" turn together.

The Syncom IV-5 communications satellite, photographed from the orbiting space shuttle *Columbia*

Figure 20. You can build a model of a Syncom satellite.

The View From Space

Astronomers have known for centuries that their view of the stars and planets would be much clearer if light from these celestial objects weren't distorted by the earth's atmosphere. Now their dreams have been realized. Several years ago the space shuttle carried the Hubble Space Telescope into an orbit well above the atmosphere. There it can not only see seven times farther into space and detect starlight undisturbed by the atmosphere, but it can also detect other types of radiation that never penetrate our atmosphere at all. Although astronauts have had to install corrective "eyeglasses" and replace wobbly solar panels on the telescope, it has provided astronomers with views of space never seen before. Among other things, it has detected young stars surrounded by dense, flattened disks of dust, confirming the idea that infant stars develop the rings of matter needed to form planets. Here is an example of a technology that is making possible new giant strides in the science of astronomy.

Astronauts working in space to repair the Hubble Space Telescope in December 1993

4

LIVING IN SPACE

In 1984, President Reagan recommended that within a decade the United States should have a permanent space station in orbit. While Space Station Freedom, a project involving Canada, Japan, and the European Space Agency, as well as the United States, will not be completed on schedule, the station is being planned. Construction is scheduled to begin in 1995. Materials needed to build the station will be transported to space by the space shuttle orbiter or by unmanned vehicles similar to the shuttle. Much of the structure will be assembled using the Canadian-built remote manipulator system, but some delicate hookups will require space-walking astronauts.

Space station technology will allow scientists to carry out experiments on the effects of prolonged weightlessness on humans, animals, and plants. Such experiments are essential to a planned three-year voyage of humans to Mars. But the station will also allow researchers to prepare crystals that do not grow well in the presence of gravity, drugs that require a weightless environment or a better vacuum than can be achieved on earth, and alloys from metals of different densities that do not mix well in earth's gravity.

To see how materials separate because of gravity, you might mix different metals. But this procedure would be dangerous because you would have to heat them to a very high temperature. You can see the same effect by mixing two liquids.

MIXING AND GRAVITY

MATERIALS
- *cooking oil*
- *small jar and cover*
- *water*

Pour cooking oil into a small jar until it is about one-third filled. Add an equal amount of water. Seal the jar and shake. What happens?

Place the jar on a counter. Stand back and observe. What happens to the liquids? Which liquid is denser (has more weight for the same volume)—water or cooking oil? How can you tell? What could you do to confirm your answer?

Electricity in Space

Each end of the space station will have giant solar panels. These panels are used to produce electricity. Sunlight falling on the panels is converted to electrical energy. Research related to the space program was essential in developing the technology of photovoltaic (solar) cells and in reducing their cost. These cells are being used more and more on earth as well as in space. Small solar cells are frequently used to power hand-held calculators. In space, arrays of solar panels provide the only practical way of producing electricity over extended periods of time. Activity 18 will show you how light can generate electricity.

ELECTRICITY FROM LIGHT

MATERIALS
- *photovoltaic cell*
- *connecting wires*
- *sunlight or light bulb*
- *sensitive ammeter (microammeter or milliammeter)*
- *voltmeter*
- *resistor*

Ask an adult to help you build the electric circuit shown in Figure 21. (Several different resistors and meters may be required to find a combination that gives measurable values.) Let sunlight or light from a bright bulb fall on the photovoltaic cell. How can you tell that electrical energy is being generated? What happens if you change the angle at which the light strikes the photocell? What angle produces the most electrical energy?

Space and Weightlessness

Although traveling to space, living there, and returning to earth is easier than it used to be, it still requires training and preparation. Astronauts and scientists in the weightlessness of space often experience nausea. Experiments are now under way to see if people can be trained to overcome this annoyance so common to space travelers.

You may wonder why people in orbit about the earth feel weightless. After all, it's the force of gravity that keeps space shuttles, space stations, and satellites in orbit. Without this inward force, the vehicle would travel along a straight-line path into deep space. You saw this in Activity 15.

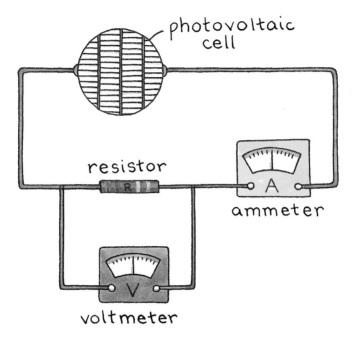

Figure 21. An electric circuit is shown in this drawing. What takes the place of a battery?

On earth, we all feel the earth pressing against our feet when we stand, or against our bottoms when we sit. In an orbiting spaceship, however, both you and the ship are pulled toward the earth. The ship's speed coupled with its continual fall toward the earth just matches the earth's curvature (refer to Figure 17). As you saw in Activity 11, all objects, regardless of their mass, have the same acceleration as they fall. It is no different in space. Both you and the ship fall toward the earth at the same rate. It's as if you were standing in a free-falling elevator. The elevator would exert no force on your feet because both you and the elevator would be falling with the same acceleration.

Demonstrating the weightless environment in the space laboratory on the *Columbia* space shuttle

A "FALLING" ELEVATOR

MATERIALS
- *spring-type bathroom scale*
- *elevator*

A free-falling elevator could be disastrous, but all "down" elevators must accelerate in that direction when they begin their downward motion. They don't fall freely, one would hope, but they do accelerate downward. To see what effect this acceleration has on your weight, take a spring-type bathroom scale into an elevator. Stand on the scale and press the down button. What happens to your weight as the elevator accelerates downward? What is your weight according to the scale when the elevator is moving at a constant speed? As it decelerates to a stop? What do you think will happen to your weight if, after the elevator stops, you push the up button and the elevator accelerates as it starts upward? How is this activity related to the weightlessness you would feel in orbit?

Although it's not easy to simulate weightlessness on earth, it is part of an astronaut's training. One way is to move about under water in a suit that allows the astronaut to float like a submarine beneath the surface. How is this like being weightless in a spaceship? How is it different?

Another approach that works for short periods of time is to fly in an airplane along the hump of a long circular arc. The plane's speed is adjusted so that its inward acceleration toward the center of the arc equals the downward acceleration of gravity.

You've probably had the sensation of weightlessness, but only for brief moments. When you jump up into the air or down from a wall or step, there is a brief time when you don't feel the earth pushing upward on your feet.

Activity 20 provides a way to obtain repeated sensations of weightlessness and brief looks at weightless conditions.

ACTIVITY 20

WEIGHTLESSNESS

MATERIALS
- *playground swing*
- *spring scale with large visible numbers*
- *object to weigh*
- *paper or Styrofoam coffee cup*
- *pencil to punch holes*
- *water*

Get on a playground swing and "pump" until you are swinging quite high. At each end of the swing, there is a brief interval when the swing exerts no force on your body. You and the swing seat are both accelerating downward at the same rate. During that short time you have the sensation of being weightless. What do you feel at the middle of your swing?

You can also see some effects that would be common in the weightless environment of a space station in orbit about the earth. Hang an object from a spring scale that has large visible numbers. How much does the object weigh?

Place a number of pillows on the floor beneath the weight. Ask a friend to hold the spring and attached weight high above the pillows. Then watch the scale when your friend releases the scale and lets the weight and scale fall onto the pillows. What is the object's weight as it falls? How much would the object appear to weigh if you weighed it on the space station?

Near the bottom of a paper or Styrofoam coffee cup, punch two holes, one on either side. Then fill the cup with water and hold it over a sink. Notice the streams of water that flow out of the cup. Fill the cup again. Put your fingers over the holes so the water can't flow out, and take the cup outside. Ask a friend to hold the cup high above the ground and let the water flow from the holes. Then, while the water is still flowing, ask your friend to drop the cup. Watch closely. Why do you think the water streams stop flowing as the cup falls?

On a space station, when you try to walk by pushing against the ship, the ship pushes back with an equal but opposite force, and you float away toward the other side of the cabin. How does this result compare with what you found in Activity 13? What might be done so that astronauts could walk along the ship easily and safely?

Eating in space is another problem. It can be very messy. As Sally Ride said after one trip aboard the space shuttle, "A few foods, like scrambled eggs, are not quite sticky enough to stay on a spoon. I quickly learned to hold the carton close to my mouth and use my spoon to aim each bite of egg."

★ ACTIVITY 21

EATING IN SPACE

MATERIALS
- *applesauce*
- *Ziploc bag*
- *scissors*
- *plastic cup*
- *water*
- *soda straw*
- *chair*

In order to avoid having food fly off spoons or plates, some of the astronauts' food comes in squeeze containers. You can make a similar container by putting some applesauce in a Ziploc plastic bag. Be sure the bag is securely closed. Then use scissors to snip off one corner of the bag. Put that open corner in your mouth and slowly squeeze the applesauce into your mouth. Why do astronauts eat this way in space?

Do astronauts need a tube that extends from container to stomach in order to eat when they are weightless? After all, in such an environment, gravity will not cause food to fall toward the stomach.

One way to answer this question is to see whether gravity is needed to move food into your stomach. You can find out by placing a water-filled plastic cup on the floor beside a chair. Put a soda straw in the cup. Then put your stomach on the seat of the chair and lean your head down toward the end of the straw. In this position, your head will be below your stomach.

Now try drinking water through the straw. Can you do it? Is gravity needed to carry food from your mouth to your stomach? If not, what does move the food to your stomach?

One way to avoid the problems associated with weightlessness is to create an artificial gravity. This can be done by making the spaceship rotate. If a disk-shaped spaceship with a radius of 10 m (32.8 ft) is rotating once every 9 seconds, the inward acceleration of the outside walls of the ship is nearly 4.9 m/s every second—about half the acceleration due to gravity on the earth. If you were to stand on this wall, you would "weigh" half as much as you do on earth; that is, you would feel the wall pushing on you with about half the force that you feel when the earth pushes upward on your feet.

If you've ever taken a ride on one of the spinning barrels found at many amusement parks, you're familiar with this artificial gravity. When the barrel is spinning at top speed, the inward force is so great that you stick to the wall. Even when the bottom of the barrel is lowered, you still don't fall. The force due to the inward-pushing wall is so strong that the friction between you and the wall keeps you in place.

ACTIVITY 22

A MODEL
OF ARTIFICIAL GRAVITY

MATERIALS
- *lazy Susan*
- *marble*

If the lazy Susan has a lip around its outer edge, you're all set. If it doesn't, you can make one by taping a narrow strip of thin cardboard to the rim. Place a marble at the rim of the lazy Susan. Then spin the lazy Susan. What happens to the marble? What keeps it moving in a circle? How does this model illustrate the artificial gravity that can be created in a spinning spaceship?

GOING FURTHER

In this book you have seen only a small portion of the science and technology involved in space programs. There is much more that you can investigate. Some of the things you might like to investigate are listed below.

★ • Why do planets and stars not move through exactly 360° during a 24-hour period?

• Lengthy human missions on a space station or on a trip to Mars will require lots of water. How can water be recycled so that only small amounts need to be lifted into space?

• There is no air in space. How will astronauts obtain oxygen during long periods in space?

★ • How might solar energy be used for cooking as well as for generating electricity?

★ • Investigate the design and nature of the space suits and Manned Maneuvering Units (MMUs) used by astronauts who "walk" in space. How do the astronauts breathe? How are their bodies cooled? How are they able to move from place to place in empty space?

★ • Bathroom scales would be useless on a space station. How could an astronaut find his or her weight (or is it mass?) in space?

- What's different about the bathrooms on a space shuttle or space station? What will be done with body wastes and the trash produced during long journeys in space?

★ - What are some of the problems astronauts face when they try to work in space? How can these problems be solved?

- Several spin-off technologies from space programs were mentioned in the Introduction. Make a more extensive list of the spin-offs from space programs. Make another list of the spin-off technology that you might anticipate during the building of a space station or a lunar station or in preparing for a trip to Mars.

- What is virtual reality? How is it related to the space program and the building of Space Station Freedom?

- What is extraterrestrial intelligence? How are space scientists searching for such intelligence? What makes them think it exists?

- What is space junk? How does it affect the space program? What can be done about it?

- Which planets have been visited by space probes? How have these space probes enhanced our knowledge of the solar system?

GLOSSARY

acceleration: an increase in the speed of an object. A decrease in speed can be referred to as deceleration or a negative acceleration. Accelerations, both positive and negative, occur only when a force is acting.

constellations: a group of stars that appear to form a fixed pattern in the sky. The stars may actually be at vastly different distances from the earth.

escape velocity: the velocity required for an object to move into deep space and never return to earth. For earth, the escape velocity is 40,000 km/hr.

friction: the force that opposes the motion of one surface over another.

geocentric: a model in which the earth is at the center of the universe and all the heavenly bodies revolve around the earth.

gravity: the force of attraction between two masses. The earth, for example, exerts a force on you that pulls you toward its center.

You, in turn, exert an equal force on the earth (the third law of motion).

heliocentric: a model in which the sun is the center of the solar system, and all planets, including the earth, revolve around the sun.

inertia: the resistance to a change in motion. The greater an object's mass, the greater will be the force required to produce a given change in its motion.

light–year: the distance light travels in one year, which is nearly six trillion (6,000,000,000,000) miles—almost 1600 times the distance from the sun to Pluto.

mass ratio: the mass of a fully fueled rocket divided by the mass of the rocket alone.

momentum: the mass of a body times its velocity.

Newton's first law of motion: objects remain in motion or at rest unless acted on by outside forces.

Newton's second law of motion: an object accelerates in the direction of the force applied to it. The greater the force, the greater the acceleration; the larger the mass, the less the acceleration.

Newton's third law of motion: for every action force there is an equal but opposite reaction force.

photovoltaic cells: devices such as those found on many pocket calculators that convert light to electrical energy.

planets: bodies that move in orbits around the sun because of their gravitational attraction toward the sun. The planets in our solar system are Mercury, Venus, Earth, Mars, Jupiter, Saturn, Uranus,

Neptune, and Pluto. The planets were originally called wanderers because their positions in the sky relative to the constellations, which remain fixed, were continually changing.

satellite: an object that revolves around a planet. The moon, for example, is a natural satellite of the earth. Space stations are artificial satellites.

space: the region that extends beyond the earth's atmosphere.

sphere: a round, three-dimensional object, such as a ball.

stars: large astronomical bodies such as the sun that emit light. The light comes from nuclear reactions that go on within the star.

weightlessness: a condition that exists when the gravitational acceleration of a space vehicle matches that of the occupants of the vehicle.

UNITS AND THEIR ABBREVIATIONS

LENGTH

English	Metric
mile (mi)	kilometer (km)
yard (yd)	meter (m)
foot (ft)	centimeter (cm)
inch (in.)	millimeter (mm)

AREA

English	Metric
square mile (mi^2)	square kilometer (km^2)
square yard (yd^2)	square meter (m^2)
square foot (ft^2)	square centimeter (cm^2)
square inch ($in.^2$)	square millimeter (mm^2)

VOLUME

English	Metric
cubic mile (mi^3)	cubic kilometer (km^3)
cubic yard (yd^3)	cubic meter (m^3)
cubic foot (ft^3)	cubic centimeter (cm^3)
cubic inch ($in.^3$)	cubic millimeter (mm^3)
ounce (oz)	liter (L)
	milliliter (mL)

MASS

English	Metric
pound (lb)	kilogram (kg)
ounce (oz)	gram (g)

TIME

hour (hr)

minute (min)

second (s)

FORCE OR WEIGHT

English

ounce (oz)

pound (lb)

Metric

newton (N)

SPEED OR VELOCITY

English

miles per hour (mi/hr)

miles per second (mi/s)

feet per second (ft/s)

Metric

kilometers per hour (km/hr)

kilometers per second (km/s)

meters per second (m/s)

centimeters per second (cm/s)

TEMPERATURE

English

degrees Fahrenheit (°F)

Metric

degrees Celsius (°C)

ENERGY

calorie (cal)

Calorie (Cal)

joule (J)

POWER

watt (W) = joule per second (J/s)

ELECTRICAL UNITS

volt (V)

ampere (A)

MATERIALS

accelerometer

air hockey game (optional)

applesauce

ball

balloons, various

bike

bit, 1.5-mm (1/16-in.)

blocks of wood

board

book

carpenter's level

chair

clear tape

clear, watertight vial

colored pens or crayons

cone

connecting wires

cooking oil

cylinder

disk

drill

empty thread spool

flashlight

globe

grooved ruler

ice skates, roller skates, or skateboards

large, identical toy trucks (2)

lazy Susan

light bulb

long, thin rubber band

marble

metal washers (various sizes)

meter stick, yardstick, or ruler

narrow-mouth jar

paper clips

paper or Styrofoam coffee cup

paper

pencil

penlight

photovoltaic cell

pins

plastic picnic plate or plastic snap-on cover

plastic cup

playing card

pulley

resistor

sandpaper

scissors

sensitive ammeter (microammeter or milliameter)

shoes, books, paperweights, etc.

small mirrors

small piece of soap

small jar and cover

smooth board about 20-30 cm (8-12 in.) wide and .6-.9 m (2-3 ft.)
    long

soda straw

spring scale with large visible numbers (borrow from school)

spring balance calibrated in newtons (0-20 N) (borrow from
    school)

spring-type clothespins

square piece of 6-mm (1/4-in.) plywood 7.5 cm (3 in.) on a side

standard masses (100 g, 200 g, 500 g, 1,000 g or 1 kg)
string
study lamp
tape
thread
thumbtacks
toothpick
turntable
twist ties
voltmeter
wagon, large enough to sit in
water
wood glue
Ziploc bag

INDEX

ABOUT THE AUTHOR

Robert Gardner, science educator and award-winning author of nonfiction for young people, has written over fifty books to introduce readers to the wonders of science. A *School Library Journal* reviewer has called him "the master of the science experiment book."

He earned a B.A. from Wesleyan University and an M.A. from Trinity College. Before retiring, he taught biology, chemistry, physics, and physical science for over thirty years at Salisbury School in Salisbury, Connecticut. He and his wife, Natalie, reside in Massachusetts where he serves as a consultant on science education and continues to write books for future scientists.